Thank you to the generous team who gave their time and talents to make this book possible:

Author
Elizabeth Spor Taylor

Illustrator
April Phillips

Creative Directors
Caroline Kurtz, Jane Kurtz,
and Kenny Rasmussen

Translator
Jekap Omod

Designer
Beth Crow

Ready Set Go Books, an Open Hearts Big Dreams Project

Special thanks to Ethiopia Reads donors and staff for believing in this project and helping get it started-- and for arranging printing, distribution, and training in Ethiopia.

ISBN: 979-8405738024
Library of Congress Control Number:2022901181

Published: 01/26/22

Who Am I?

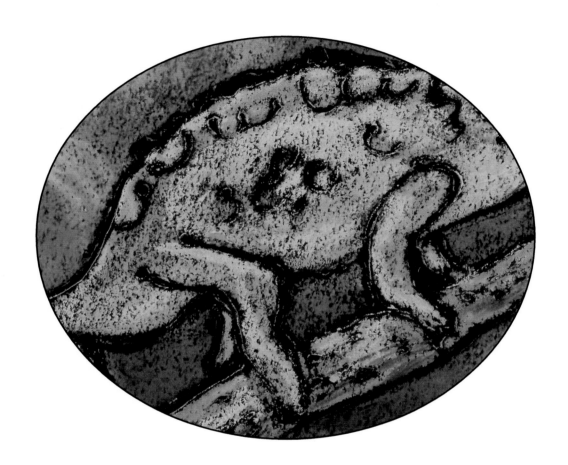

Aana Nga?

English and Anuak

Let's play a game.
Do you know these animals?

**O kwäägø ki kwääk aciel.
Lääy moi ngäyi?kana beektu?**

Who am I? Aana nga?

Here is my black mane.

Moi bee jïëc nguta moa cøl.

Can you see my bushy tail?

Jïba mana no onyijuk nëënö jïrï?

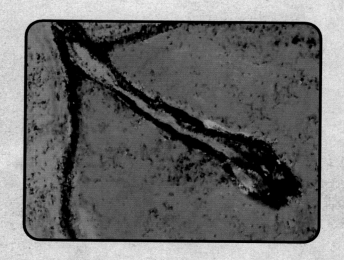

I hunt at night.

A dwar ki wäär.

I am a black-maned lion.

Aana nguu mana jïëc ngute cøl.

Who am I?   Aana nga?

Here are my striped legs.

Moi bee tieta moa näk akïti kïti.

Can you see my black eye?

Nyengnga moa cøl nëënö jïrï?

I eat grass.

Acämö ki luum.

I am a Somali wild donkey.

Aana arëën paap mar Comaali.

Who am I?   Aana nga?

Here is my brown nose.

**Man bee uma
mana na agïira.**

Can you see my gray fur?

**Jïër moa no obwörö
mooa nëënö jïrï?**

I live in bamboo trees.

Abëëdö yïth böölle.

I am a Bale Mountains vervet.

Aano ongweerø mar kïn Baale.

Who am I?

Aana nga?

Here are my small ears.

Moi bee ïththa moa therø.

Can you see my pointy nose?

Uma mana beth nëënö jïrï?

Many people call me a fox.

Jiy mo thööth acøørge no othöö.

I am an Ethiopian wolf.

Aano othöö mar Ithïöpia.

Who am I?   ## Aana nga?

Here is my blue eye.

Man bee wanga mana lïw.

Can you see my curled tail?

Jïba man ni ree døøllø en nëënö jïrï?

I change color.

Kït mooa willa willø.

I am a heather chameleon.

Aano ongøønnø.

Who am I?

Aana nga?

Here is my yellow head.

Man bee wiïa mana näk abäga.

Can you see my green wing?

Böömma mana mar nëënö jirï?

I eat fruit.

Acämö ki nyïï jenni.

I am a yellow-fronted parrot.

Aana paaröt mana näk täär nyïme abäga.

Who am I?   Aana nga?

Here are my horns.

Moi bee tuungï moa.

Can you see my striped fur?

Jïër moa moi no okewø en nëënö jïrï?

I bark.

A guyö

I am a mountain nyala.

Aana Nyala mar bäät kïdi.

Who am I? Aana nga?

Here are my white teeth.

Lak moi ni tar ii
bee mooa.

Can you see my black nose?

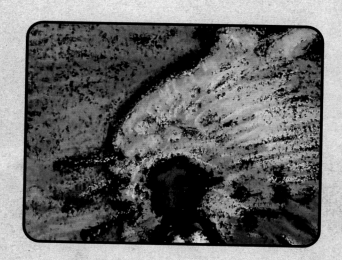

Uma mana cøl
nëënö jïrï?

I dig tunnels.

Akunyö ki buri.

I am a big-headed mole rat.

Aana jïïö mana wïïe dwøng (adula).

Who am I?   Aana nga?

Here is my red chest.

Man bee kööra mana kwaar.

Can you see my black eyes?

Nyengnga moa cøl nëënö jïrï?

I sleep on cliffs.

Abuuta bäät kïte.

I am a gelada baboon.

Aana ajwøm mar gëlaada.

Who am I?   Aana nga?

Here is my red beak.

Man bee dhaa mana kwaar.

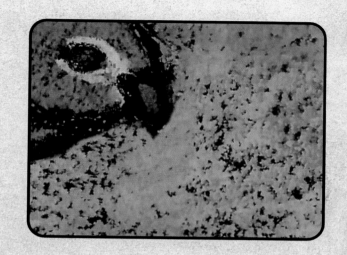

Can you see my blue tail?

Jïba mana lïw nëënö jïrï?

I fly from tree to tree.

Amäädö bäät jenni.

I am a Prince Ruspoli's Turaco.

Aana winyø mo cwøl ni kwääny rucpölïc turkö.

Play again!
Tell your friends about all these amazing animals.

Cang kwääk! Luum lääy moi ni mïërö bëët ii caani jï nyïa wäätu.

About The Story

The animals in this book live only in Ethiopia and nowhere else. One of the most fascinating is the Ethiopian wolf, the rarest wolf in the world and one of only a handful of wolf species in Africa. Many Ethiopians know the animal as the Simien fox. Though it is larger than a fox, there are many characteristics that make it similar. Like a fox, the Ethiopian wolf has red fur, a bushy tail, long legs, a white throat patch, black markings, a long muzzle, and pointed ears. But DNA samples confirm it is directly related to the grey wolf.

Interestingly, Ethiopian wolves and gelada baboons have a symbiotic relationship. Gelada baboons allow Ethiopian wolves to hunt within their herds. When doing so, Ethiopian wolves are twice as likely to capture their prey.

With less than 500 adults alive today, the Ethiopian wolf is the most endangered carnivore in Africa. Since 1995, the Ethiopian Wolf Conservation Programme has collaborated with the Ethiopian government and local communities to protect the Ethiopian wolf. www.ethiopianwolf.org

About The Author

Elizabeth Spor Taylor is an international literacy specialist who served as writer and editor of English learning materials for Ethiopian students. She has traveled to Ethiopia eleven times visiting schools and working collaboratively with Ethiopian educators throughout the country.

Elizabeth became familiar with the successes of Ethiopia Reads while touring sponsored libraries in various regions of Ethiopia. Her expertise is in primary grades literacy relative to native English speakers as well as English Speakers of Other Languages.

She is a contributing member of the Book Centered Learning Committee for Ethiopia Reads and supports the advancement of English skills within the immigrant and refugee population in Cleveland, Ohio.

About the Illustrator

April Phillips' lifelong love for art, both classic and modern, was handed down from her uniquely talented mother. Taking that inspiration, April hopes to inspire another generations' love of art with her book illustrations and teaching.

About Open Hearts Big Dreams

Open Hearts Big Dreams began as a volunteer organization, led by Ellenore Angelidis in Seattle, Washington, to provide sustainable funding and strategic support to Ethiopia Reads, collaborating with Jane Kurtz. OHBD has now grown to be its own nonprofit organization supporting literacy, innovation, and leadership for young people in Ethiopia.

Ellenore Angelidis comes from a family of teachers who believe education is a human right, and opportunity should not depend on your birthplace. And as the adoptive mother of a little girl who was born in Ethiopia and learned to read in the U.S., as well as an aspiring author, she finds the chance to positively impact literacy hugely compelling!

About Ready Set Go Books

Reading has the power to change lives, but many children and adults in Ethiopia cannot read. One reason is that Ethiopia doesn't have enough books in local languages to give people a chance to practice reading. Ready Set Go books wants to close that gap and open a world of ideas and possibilities for kids and their communities.

When you buy a Ready Set Go book, you provide critical funding to create and distribute more books.

Learn more at: http://openheartsbigdreams.org/book-project/

Ready Set Go 10 Books

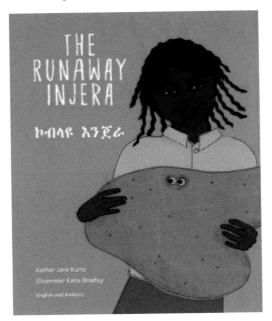

In 2018, Ready Set Go Books decided to experiment by trying a few new books in larger sizes.

Sometimes it was the art that needed a little more room to really shine. Sometimes the story or nonfiction text was a bit more complicated than the short and simple text used in most of our current early reader books.

We called these our "Ready Set Go 10" books as a way to show these ones are bigger and also sometimes have more words on the page. The response has been great so now our Ready Set Go 10 books are a significant number of our titles. We are happy to hear feedback on these new books and on all our books.

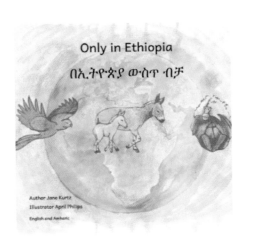

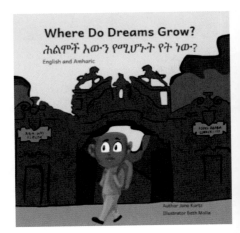

About the Language

Dha-Anywaa is spoken by the Anyuak people also known as Anywaae, Anuak and Anyuak. Anyuak are part of the larger Luo Nilothic ethnic group from the "Western Nilotes". They live along the rivers Gilo, Agwey, Dikony, Akobo, Nyikani, Oboth, Alworo, and Openo in the Eastern part of the Southern Sudan and in Southwest Ethiopia.

About the Translation

Jekap Omod was born and raised in Gambella, Ethiopia. In 2014, Jekap and his family moved to the US and attended Austin High school. He graduated with his Bachelor degree in Neuroscience from the University of Minnesota in 2021.

Jekap currently works as a researcher in the medical department at the University of Minnesota. He is passionate about his research which focuses on understanding the impact of stress and anxiety on the brain. He plans to apply for medical school and become a surgeon. In his free time, Jekap loves to play piano and mentor kids. He also makes short videos, teaching Dha-Anywaa to kids.

To view all available titles, search "Ready Set Go Ethiopia" or scan QR code

 Chaos

 Talk Talk Turtle

 The Glory of Gondar

 We Can Stop the Lion

 Not Ready!

 Fifty Lemons

 Count For Me

 Too Brave

 Tell Me What You Hear

Open Heart Big Dreams is pleased to offer discounts for bulk orders, educators and organizations.

Contact ellenore@openheartsbigdreams.org for more information.

Made in the USA
Middletown, DE
15 February 2022